OCTOBOY and the GRILLES

"Kids Say the Darndest"
Things for the Digital Age

P.R. Brown

Octoboy & The Grilles
Copyright © 2022 by P. R. Brown

ISBN
978-1-959314-69-1 (Paperback)
978-1-959314-70-7 (eBook)

A Little Background

In 2009, at the tender age of 51, I was thrust into a new phase of my life, "Papa Hood". Now I'm a singer - songwriter, a rock n roll kind of guy and there was no way that I was going to be called "grampa". In fact, I would have preferred to just be called "Pete", but Papa is what we finally settled on.

For some unknown reason, I've always given the kids nick names. I have four beautiful daughters: Pam (Charles), Jill (Willie), Jessica (Bob) and Stephanie (Stevers). I have five granddaughters: Rosie (Bratface), Mary Kay (Blondie), Kaiya (Pudgers), Gracie (Grayson), and Eve (Pudgesickle). And I also have one Grandson, Norbie aka Octoboy.

Somewhere along the line, about 5 years ago we became the designated day care center for Jill's kids, Rosie, Mary Kay and Norbie. Pamela is Kaiya's mom and they live in Colorado, so we only get to see them a couple of times a year. Stephanie's kids, Grace and Eve go to regular Day Care. But we have the other three after school every day, and all week on School vacations.

Two years ago, OctoBoy's day care center lost it's lease where they operated, which left Jill scrambling to find somewhere else to take him, which was hard because it was November and all of the other facilities were already full. She could only find one place with any openings and that was only for two days a week. By now, I think you can surmise where he was going to go for those other three days. I forgot to mention that anytime there's no school, Holidays, Teacher Conference days, Spring Break, Winter Break and Summer Vacation, all three of them have been coming here, so basically, Roni and I are co-raising them.

Norbie and I have had a tight bond right from day one. Maybe it's the testosterone in a world full of estrogen. When he first learned to talk, he would sit there and sing "Papa, Papa, Papa", over and over again. When Jill would pick up the girls and he was in the car seat, he would yell for me until I came out to see him. If there was a party, he would run across the room to me as soon as I walked in the door. One year at Christmas, we were all together at my brother's house. I was in the kitchen holding Grace and Norbie, who wasn't even two yet, waddled into the room and didn't like what he saw. He bee lined across the kitchen floor and began pounding my knee caps with his pudgy little paws. He didn't like the fact that another little kid was getting my attention!

Now in our age of social media, I would often post things to FaceBook, that the kids had said or done that were either cute or just down right hysterical, mostly just to share what happened with out of town relatives. I never thought much about it at the time, but I always had comments from folks who were amused by them. More and more, people would say "You should write a book about these things". For a long time, I just shrugged it off. I figured there was no way I could ever remember all of the crazy things they did or said. But then a few months ago, I was poking around my FaceBook page and found that they were all there.

Everything I had posted was chronicled by date and right there at my finger tips for me to cut, paste and print.

And as for the name OctoBoy, it's not that he's a super hero or that he has any sort of physical abnormality. It's because right from the time he gained motor skills, he's had the fastest hands of any kid I've ever seen. It was as though he had eight hands! One day while I was holding him, he managed to knock my glasses off and spill my wine with one hand and pull the chain off of my neck with the other, all at the same time. And "grilles" is just the crazy little way he says "girls."

So there you have it; OctoBoy & The Grilles. I hope you laugh as hard as we did.

March 6, 2012

So I popped into Jill's tonight and had her pop my new song, "Honey Come With Me". into her CD player. Jill and Mary Kay danced together while Rosie went crazy, dancing and singing in her own little world. Every time it ended, she went over and replayed it while Jill had gone to draw a bath for the girls, but Rosie wasn't interested. She grabbed my finger to dance and said, "Papa! That's you singing! Mon, dance with me!" I'll call that a good day!

May 30, 2012

Mary Kay listens very well for a 1 year old. Several times yesterday, I would say "no-no" and she would stop right away. The only problem was that when I would say it, she would start shaking her head back and forth, get herself dizzy and fall over!

July 11, 2012

So last night, Rosie told Jill: "Mom, we need to get a new baby. This one is weird." That kid has NO business calling anyone else weird.

August 10, 2012

Poor little Brat Face gets her tonsils and adenoids taken out today. Good thing she's got Aunts like this!

October 30, 2012

So my phone just rang.

Me: Hello?

Rosie: Papa?

Me: Hello Bratface!

Rosie: Know what?

Me: Tell me.

Rosie: I don't want Obama. I want the other President

Me: You're a smart girl!

Rosie: I know. Bye Papa.

Then all I could hear was her Mom laughing in the background!

March 2, 2013

I am officially disowning Rosie. I asked her if she liked The Beatles. She told me that beetles are gross. I told her, not the bugs, the ones that sing. She said "There's beetles that can sing?" So I pulled up a video of "She Loves You" on YouTube. She told me "Turn that off, I don't like it". Nice knowin' ya, Kid".

June 24, 2013

Here's a conversation from yesterday:

Rosie: I'm 6 (no idea why she said that)

Me: I thought you were 3.

Rosie: No, I'm 6. Wait, I mean 16. And I can drive now. So I can drive you anywhere. And you're my husband and your name is Nick. And my name is Elysha. And I have 2 daughters. One is 6 and one is 5.

Me: So I'm your husband, you're 16 and you have a 5 & a 6 year old?

Rosie: Yes.

Me: You're just all kindsa trailer park, aren't ya kid?

Rosie: Yes. Could you get me a beer Hun?

I picked the wrong day to quit sniffing glue.

November 24, 2013

I asked Rosie who was babysitting last night. She said "Uncle John. But not the armpit tickling one. The one that comes from Gramma Duncan's house"

Bratface's first foray into meatball making.

I gave her a lemon wedge, expecting the kind of reaction you would get from most kids. Not this one. She ate the fruit from inside of it and wanted another one.

March 10, 2014

So the other night when Jill was here with the kids, Mary Kay comes running across the room toward me with her arms up for me to pick her up. I get her in my arms, she pushes my glasses up on top of my head and starts to rub the palms of her hands all over my face.

Her: Where you whiskers?

Me: I shaved them off.

Her: Go shave them back on. They tickle my hands.

I never thought of that.

July 7, 2014

So my mother and I pull into my sister's house who had my grandkids there. Mary Kay saw me and ran off the porch, across the lawn and jumped into my arms. She felt my face and said "Papa, I can't believe you here, is it really you?" She didn't want me to put her down and after we went inside, she said "Papa? Does your back hurt?" I smiled and said that it was fine. She gave me a grin and said "good" and wrapped her arms around my neck, even tighter. Not sure where that came from, but I'll take it.

August 2, 2014

Me: Mary Kay, what do you want for lunch?

Mary Kay: (pauses for a second, tilts her head and puts her index finger on her chin) Peanut butter and chicken

Sounds about right.

September 16, 2014

Another foray in brat sitting:

> Rosie: Papa, whose gum is that?
>
> Me: Mine. Whose did you think it was
>
> Rosie: I dont know. It couldda been Gramma Roni's
>
> Me: Ok, good point
>
> Rosie: Could I have a piece?
>
> Me: You could if I let you.
>
> Rosie: Will you let me?
>
> Me: Sure kiddo. Here ya go. Just make sure when you're done with it that it goes into the toilet.
>
> Rosie: Thank you! (and runs into the other room)

Mary Kay was in the living room, heard Rosie saying thank you and runs into the kitchen and says "Papa, can I please have..(long pause) whatever Rosie has?"

> Me: She has a strange personality disorder.
>
> Mary Kay: Can I have one too, please?

Trust me kid, you already have one. Never a dull moment with those two around. They make me laugh more than Ron White does.

September 25, 2014

Last Tuesday, I picked Rosie up from school and she stayed with me for the rest of the day until Jill got home from work. Got her a little snack and we decided to take a walk around the block. As we're walking, totally out of the blue, she says "Papa, we don't like Obama, right?" I held back my laughter and asked her where that came from. And the response was "We like Womney" She just turned 5 and the election was two years ago. If ya think kids don't pay attention....

October 6, 2014, OctoBoy entered our lives. He was born on a Monday and Mom stood up in her baby sister Stephanie's wedding on Saturday. We all soon realized that it was his world and the rest of us were allowed to be in it. He was only a couple of months old when he got sick with RSV and landed in the hospital for two days. This was one of the saddest photos I'd ever seen.

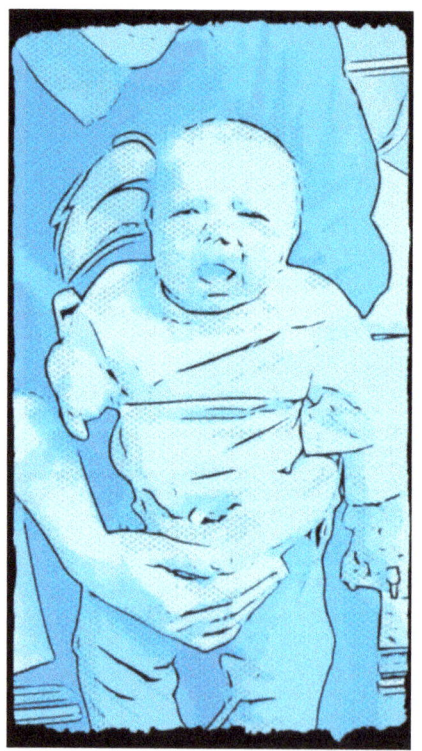

November 11, 2014

Mary Kay: Who's my godmother?

Me: I am.

Mary Kay: No Papa, you a boy.

Me: Want a Kit Kat?

Mary Kay: Yeth please

Mary Kay: You still a boy.

Yep, it's still there. Just checkin'.

November 18, 2014

He was wailing the other day and I told Mary Kay to teach him to suck his thumb. I was only kidding.

December 13, 2014

Rosie was here the other day and she was sitting across from me while I was putting some things in the dishwasher. She stares at what I'm doing and asks "Papa, why are you putting those dishes away without washing them?"

Here's Norbie with Aunt Jessie on his first Christmas. But this is before he was OctoBoy. Back then, I took a lot of heat because I referred to him as Fat Boy. The kid was a lug! It didn't matter. We became, and still are best buddies!

They decided that an impromptu concert was in order.

February 8, 2015

All during the Christening service today, Mary Kay kept walking down the left aisle and making her way over to get to me. Steph says to me, "Wow Dad, Mary Kay sure likes to be with you. She's come over to you about 6 times in a half hour." And she did. Because I was feeding her mints. At one point, she reached into my coat pocket and pulled out my cigarettes and said "Papa, that your smokes. Where your candy?"

He was pretty aggravated that there was only one steak left!

April 3, 2015

So I take the girls for a walk around the block. Mary Kay says to me:

"Papa, I gotta hold your hand so no one steals me. If they did, you could sneak into their house cause they don't know you. Then you could get a knife from someone you know. Then you could cut them all up and save me and take me home and we could have a play date and you could have a beer for saving me".

One hell of an imagination on that kid.

The Michelin Tire Man!

FEED ME!

Hippie Chicks!

July 9, 2015

Just asked Mary Kay if her hands were clean. She looked at me incredulously and said (with an attitude) "Yeah, I wiped them on your jeans". Stupid me.

Did you bring the pizza?

August 13, 2015

One thing I forgot about having little kids around, you never really have a meal. You just finish whatever they don't eat.

August 13, 2015

I was just handed a piece of paper with scribbling all over it by an almost six year old curmudgeon. She told me "Here's a song I made up for your band to play. That'll be $100 please. If you don't have cash, I take credit cards." I think she's gonna do alright for herself.

September 3, 2015

For anyone who's following this, today was my last day with the kids before they go back to school. Around 4:30, I went into the garage to have a cigarette. Mary Kay wanted to come out and said "Papa, put your arm around me. I don't want to go back to school, I want to stay here with you" I'm pretty sure you can understand the pile of mush I was after that.

Well, for his sake, I hope this is true!

Lemme at em!

"You said we were going for ice cream!"

December 3, 2015

Mary Kay: "Papa? Your toothbrush jumped off the sink and fell in the toilet"

Good thing I like that kid.

December 3, 2015

My little prodigy decided to haul my music stand upstairs today and write a song. She told her sister to get away from her song pages and let her work.

I think she's spending too much time with me.

December 15, 2015

Me: Gonna watch the Republican Presidential Debate tonight?

Rosie: No. Mom won't let me. It's on too late and I have school tomorrow.

Me: Who do you want for the next President?

Rosie: I don't know. There's like 20 of them running. I know who I DON'T want it to be, And it's a GIRL!

Me: Like your sister?

Rosie: No, like HILLARY!

Not bad for a 6 year old. And for the record, I did nothing to influence her!

January 14, 2016

Rosie: I don't feel like I'm 6. I feel like I'm still 5.

Me: I know what ya mean. I still feel like I'm 18.

Rosie: Well, you're NOT 18!

Me: How old am I?

Rosie: You're at least like 27 or somethin'

I'll take that.

January 14, 2016

Think she was happy to see me?

February 4, 2016

I get Bratface off the bus yesterday. She opens the car door and before she even gets in the car, she says:

Oh my God, what a day. It was horrible. It's no wonder I get headaches.

> Me: Why? What happened?
>
> Her: Don't even ask, I don't want to talk about it.
>
> Me: Ok, I won't
>
> Her: Why? You don't want to know what happened?
>
> Me: Sure I do. Tell me what happened.
>
> Her: I don't want to talk about it.
>
> Me: Ok, then don't tell me.
>
> Her: You boys are all alike.
>
> Me: Ok, then tell me.
>
> Her: I told you not to ask, I don't want to talk about it!

February 8, 2016

Here was the "after the bus" conversation on the ride home

Bratface: Guess what? On Valentime's day, we're going to a party and then to Outback

Me: Outback? Why ya goin there?

Bratface: Oooh, it's so good! It's my favorite place!

Me: What's your favorite thing to get there?

Bratface: That's easy. The water. Yep, they have really great water there. And I'm not kiddin!
Cheap date.

Sometimes, I got "love" notes.

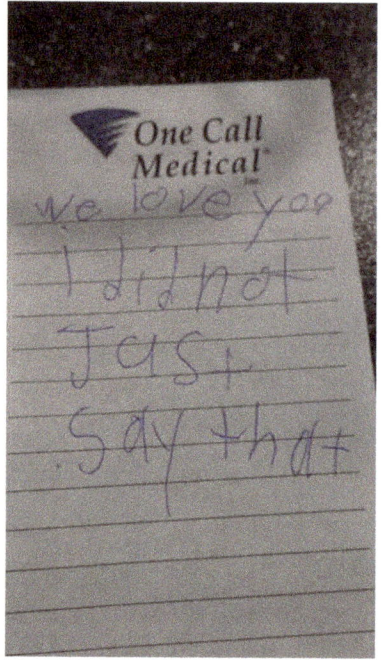

March 23, 2016

    Mary Kay: Papa?

    Me: Yes, my little blonde weirdo?

    Mary Kay: I love you. HA HA! Just kidding!

I get no respect!

March 25, 2016

5 days straight of the Disney Channel for 8 hours a day. I'm pretty much ready to blow my brains out.

March 27, 2016

This dude is stylin!! (I think I need to help him with his color coordination though)

March 28, 2016

This little Chicklette cracks me up! SO many captions that would fit this picture! I don't know how Stephanie caught this, but the timing was perfect. (So was the caption on the bib!)

April 7, 2016

It's not about just *eating* spaghetti, it's about HOW to eat it. I've got some work to do here.

May 11, 2016

So the other day, Ron fixed Brat Face a snack of something she had bought for her. Brat Face starts chowing it down.

Ron: I guess you like it, huh?

Rosie: MIND. BLOWN.

I don't know where she comes up with this stuff.

Just threw this one in because it's funny. Stephanie and Jason recreating a scene from 101 Dalmatians (with Bratface looking on in the background)

Ya never know what's going to come out of her mouth, but it's probably gonna make you laugh. Happy Birthday Mary Kay!

May 21, 2016

He saw a bird and thought he'd go play with it.

May 21, 2016

OctoBoy enjoying his favorite coffee.

June 9, 2016

I've never smelled Mustard Gas, but I changed a diaper today that had to be worse than that. A skunk's ass in my face would have been better. This was so heinous that my eyes, nose and throat burned. Vile, toxic, lethal. Any longer would have been worse than Anthrax. I put it in the garbage outside and the flies in the can died.

July 18, 2016

How do you respond when a 5 year old cocks her head sideways, raises one eyebrow when she looks at you and says "seriously dude?"

July 20, 2016

For lunch, I heated up a square piece of pizza for Mary Kay and cut it into 3 slices. She looked at it and said:

Can you cut these in half?

> Me: Then you'd have 6 pieces.
> Her: Oh. Never mind then. I can't eat that much. I'll just eat the 3.

July 25, 2016

Mary Kay to Rosie:
I wish Momma only had me. Then I could turn 15 first.

August 10, 2016

Mary Kay: This is my sleeping mask.

Me: Why do you need a sleeping mask?

Mary Kay: In case I don't feel like looking at Rosie's face.

I guess I should have known that.

August 12, 2016

Rosie made me a checklist for tomorrow so I don't forget anything for the gig.

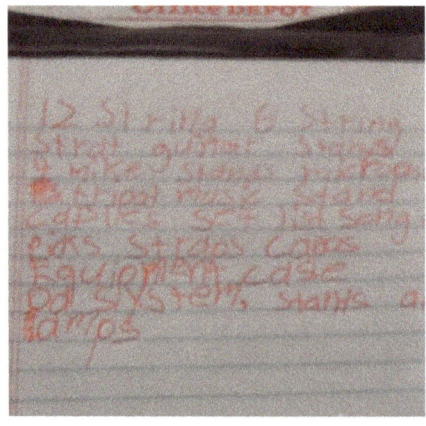

August 21, 2016

The other day I was warming something in the microwave. It beeped the normal 3 times when the time was up. But I was doing something and didn't get it out right away, so it beeped three more times. Mary Kay said "Aren't you gonna answer that thing?"

September 2, 2016

I think they've been hanging around me too long. This was the exchange this morning:

Rosie: Mary Kay, close your mouth when you chew. You sound like a slob.

Mary Kay: Yeah? Well you sound like a slob when you drink.

Rosie: I think you got your table manners at the zoo!

Me? I sat back and laughed my butt off. I wonder where they heard things like that?

September 7, 2016

Rosie: Papa, you got so much cool stuff here, guitars, pianos and drums. Why can't I play with them?

Me: Because they're instruments. Not toys. They cost tens of thousands of dollars.

Rosie: I want to go to Aunt Jeannie's. She's more fun than you.

September 19, 2016

Me: Mary Kay, what did you have for lunch today at school?

She: Chicken nuggets with broccoli and clowiefather.

I was laughing so hard, I had to pull over.

December 20, 2016

Me: What did you have for lunch today?

Bratface: Cornflakes.

Me: Cornflakes? Why?

Bratface: They had hamburgers today. They were plain with not even any mustard.

Me: Did you ask for any?

Bratface: No, those lunch ladies are very angry and mean. They're even meaner than you are Papa.

December 29, 2016

So I was downstairs about an hour ago, working on some new melody ideas. Bratface came down and was listening and asked if she could have the blue kitar on the wall. I said that it's a ukulele, but she said she could play it any way. Then she told me:

"Papa, get your kitar. I'm gonna play a song that I just maked up in my head. Play along with me and try and keep up with the rhythm".

Okay, kiddo. And yes, I laughed.

March 13, 2017

Me: You want a beer to go with those potato chips?

Mary Kay: If beer means chocolate milk, then yes I do.

March 16, 2017

Tonsils and adenoids out tomorrow. Surgery isn't until 2 and she can't eat after midnight. I'm not worried about the surgery, I'm worried about her appetite.

March 24, 2017

Every day when Brat face gets in the car, I ask her what she had for lunch. Most of the time, she tells me cereal because she didn't like what they were serving. Today, gets in and hands me this because it would have been too much to remember.

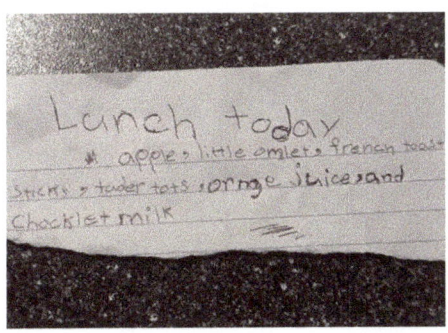

With his little Buffalo Bills cap in hand, he didn't like that the flag had fallen over.

So this Little dude came over yesterday. He crawls up into chair left, looks at me and points to the chair on the right and says "Mon Papa, let's talk".

May 17, 2017

My sister and my granddaughter share the same birth date.

May 26, 2017

So Bratface got the idea from her great gramma to write a book of all the evil things I apparently do to her. Like putting cheerios in her queso dip, or the fact that today, she was dancing in the driveway and I locked all the doors and put the garage door down while she was yelling "Hey! Let me in!". She handed me the first pages today. It's called "My Life With My Evil Papa". Then she tried to charge me $1 for reading it. Sounds like it could be a Lifetime Movie.

June 5, 2017

Another kid thing.

> Me: Hey Mary Kay, how are things since your tonsils were taken out.
>
> Mary Kay: I don't know Papa, look (opens wide}
>
> Me: Holy Crap! They grew back!
>
> Mary Kay: They did? What happens now?
>
> Me: You have to have them taken out again. You DO know that they grow from eating candy, right? You have to go through an operation again, but after that, you either have to give up candy, or keep having surgery. What do you want to do?
>
> Mary Kay: I want to wait till Gramma gets home. I don't trust you.

I tried!

June 15, 2017

> Me: Rosie, hold your head over the plate. You're spilling all over the place.
>
> Rosie: Don't you worry about it Pretty Boy.
>
> Me: What did you just say?
>
> Rosie: (uncontrollable giggling)!

June 20, 2017

So this was today's little bit of craziness on the way home from school.

Rosie: Papa, you're really weird because you smoke

Mary Kay: Leave him alone. He's BEAUTIFUL!

Me: What did you just say?

Followed by uncontrollable giggling from the back seat. I need a new job.

June 21, 2017

Free thinker.

June 23, 2017

Best thing ever. I walked into Pam's birthday party, hadda be 50 people there and one by one, Rosie, Mary Kay, Norbie and Gracie all came running when they saw me yelling "Papa! Papa!!" Never had my legs hugged so much. Yeah, I pretty much melted.

June 30, 2017

Roni took the girls to WalMart to get outfits for something. While they were there, she decided to get a kiddie pool. They checked out and took the cart back to her SUV and had Rosie and Mary Kay holding on to the pool because it was pretty windy. They got to Roni's truck and realized that it wouldn't fit. Roni told the girls they were going to have to take it back in and return it. There was a kindly couple with a pickup truck who overheard it and asked Roni, "Where do you have to go? I can take it." Roni explained that we only lived about 300 yards away, so the couple threw the pool in the back and followed them home. In the car, Roni said "Oh crap, I don't have any cash for a tip, all I have is checks."

Norbie and I heard noise outside and went to the garage. Saw Roni and the kids and an unfamiliar pickup truck. I went out and Roni explained what happened and grabbed the pool and brought it in. While I'm doing that, Mary Kay gets out of the back seat and yells "Hey Mister, my Gramma doesn't have cash for a tip. Do you want a check or should we take you to lunch at McDonalds?

July 6, 2017

Took Rosie to the Pediatrician today for an earache. The doctor checked the usual things and all was okay. Mary Kay is sitting to my left and I asked the Doctor if she had a test for little kids who can hear, but don't listen. Mary Kay's head snapped toward me so fast that I felt a breeze. The Dr. smiled and said "No tests, just shots". I asked if I should schedule it at the reception desk and the Dr. said "Yep, tell them you're with me". Mary Kay's jaw dropped, her eyes as big as saucers and said "Please Papa, I don't want a shot, I'll be good, I promise!" Point, set & match to Papa. AND the Doctor!

July 11, 2017

Mary Kay: Papa, why do you wear your hair like a girl?

Me: What do you mean?

Mary Kay: It's really long.

Me: That's because some girls like to wear their hair like guys with long hair. Jesus and The Apostles all had long hair. And some guys like to wear their hair short just like some girls prefer short hair too Mary Kay: Oh. Ok. But from the back seat, your hair is really long.

I can't win.

July 13, 2017

I refuse to let the Bratz watch any of the crap that's on Disney and Nickelodeon. Back in April, I found Sabrina The Teenage Witch on Amazon and they watched all 7 seasons. Now, they're hooked on The Cosby Show. The only problem I have with that is explaining to them what a pager, a wall mounted telephone, a station wagon and a typewriter are.

July 17, 2017

I didn't see this coming today. Lost another tooth!

July 19, 2017

So today, I have all 3 of them here. Mary Kay tell Norbie:" Ok, these are the rules at this house - don't lean on the screens, no screaming or yelling, don't get finger marks on the glass or walls, don't stand on the furniture, hold your head over the plate when you eat, when Papa tells you something, just say ok, don't ask why and use your manners". Funny how she knows the rules - but doesn't follow them.

July 19, 2017

In the midst of the mayhem, I had already scheduled a service call with Spectrum because of internet problems. He showed up right on time and Fat Boy looks at him and says

"Ow you da cayboo guy?" The guy smiles and says yes, to which Fat Boy replies "Oh. What ith you Momth name and where ow you toolth?" (Translation: "Are you the cable guy? What is your Mom's name and where are your tools?") I'll never figure out what makes kids say the things they do.

July 19, 2017

Alfalfa

July 26, 2017

So, I've got that goin' for me.

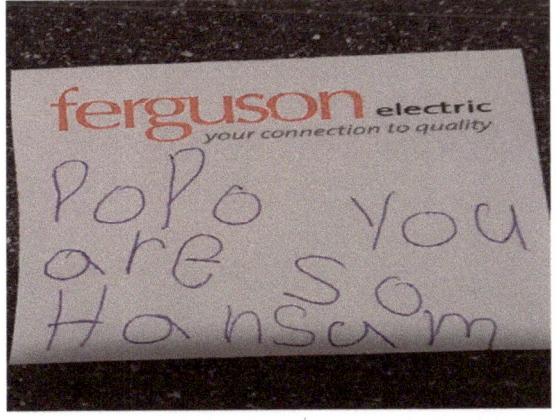

August 2, 2017

Me: Mary Kay, why did you bring a paper cup from home with you?

Mary Kay: Because you always do everything for everybody and I thought you'd be happy to not have to wash another glass.

Ok kid, ya got me.

August 3, 2017

I guess there's some animated kid's movie named Sing. I had youtube on the TV today and Bratface switches to some clips from it and tells me about some songs she discovered in it and says "You have to hear some of these songs, they're great" and then proceeds to play Under Pressure, I'm Still Standing, Eye of The Tiger and Sir Duke. Yeah, I may have heard them a time or two.

August 9, 2017

Her Royal Weirdness.

Just when I thought the day couldn't get any better, I had given Mary Kay a wet wash cloth to wipe off the sunscreen she put on when she went out for the pool. After she got rid of the bathing suit, she came in and told me she did me a favor. She took the wash cloth, laden with sunscreen, and "washed off your living room tables with it"

August 10, 2017

Me: Mary Kay, what do you want for lunch?

Mary Kay: A peanut butter and jelly sandwich without the peanut butter, please.

Me: So you want a jelly sandwich?

Mary Kay: No, I want a peanut butter and jelly sandwich without the peanut butter.

I threw in the towel.

August 15, 2017

So I get this yesterday morning.

"Papa, I had a sleepover at Gramma's on Saturday. She offered to make me breakfast, but I told her I could make my own because I learned from watching you make it for me."

August 16, 2017

Me: Mary Kay, why can I only find one of your flip flops?

Mary Kay: Because I took one home, in case I needed it.

Me: Well, why didn't you take them both home?

Mary Kay: In case I needed one here. What don't you understand about that?

August 24, 2017

So Bratface is watching R.L. Stine's Haunting Hour and tells me "This is like Gramma's killing movies (referring to Lifetime) but for kids." Yeah, that sounds about right.

August 25, 2017

Here's the most recent Mary Kay Moment and it's probably the funniest one of the summer. Yeah, there's still a few days left before School starts, but this one is hard to beat.

I'm sitting on the steps in the garage while they're playing in the driveway. Mary Kay picks up a jump rope and starts swinging it in circles, coming very close to hitting Rosie. I barked at her and she dropped the rope, walks toward me and up the steps I'm sitting on. She puts her hand on my shoulder, leans down and in a very soft voice says to me "Hang in there, Buddy. It'll be alright." And scurried away giggling. Me? I had to laugh!

August 30, 2017

Today, we're driving to my Mother's house and decided that the last day they're with me is going to be a Beatles day. We're all going to wear our Beatles shirts, listen to Beatles songs, watch Yellow Submarine and have Fish and Chips for lunch.

Rosie: Who was in that band again? I only remember hearing about Paul and John

Me: Yep, John, Paul, George and Ringo

Mary Kay: RINGO? What kinda name is that? That's a funny name!

Rosie: I know they don't play anymore, but what was the last song they did?

Me: Coincidentally, it was the last song on their last album. The name of the song was "The End"

Rosie: What's an album?

Me: Nothing you would understand, but it was called "Let It Be."

Rosie: I LOVE Let It Be!

Me: Do you know who wrote it?

Mary Kay: I think it was Jesus.

I REALLY have my work cut out for me!

August 30, 2017

So the other morning over breakfast, Bratface tells me "we were over at Papa Duncan's on Saturday and Mary Kay got in a fight with Haley". I said "Ooh, I bet he yelled at them" To which she tells me "Nah. He never yells. Neither does Gramma Duncan, Gramma Mary or Grampa Steve. It's pretty much only you that always freaks out on us"

So I got that goin' for me!

September 11, 2017

Oh my. This was when OctoBoy started staying with me on a regular basis Mary Kay's decided she was going to give him the lay of the land. Her advice was this:

1. Norbie, If papa yells, he doesn't mean it. He just wants to make sure you're safe.

2. Norbie, Papa yells a lot!

3. When he tells you to finish your plate, you don't have to. He will.

4. It doesn't matter if you're good or bad, he'll give you a freezie pop until Gramma gets home.

5. PRAY for Gramma Roni to get home. She's nice. He isn't!
So, that's my life.

September 12, 2017

So the little dude gets dropped off this morning. I tell him that we're going to do guy stuff all day and he seemed pretty stoked about that. Then something went horribly wrong

Me: Lets watch something manly on TV. Do ya wanna watch The Godfather? Die Hard? Lethal Weapon?

Him: Dora The Explorer or Barney.

Thank God he progressed to Paw Patrol!

September 14, 2017

Me: Do you have to go to the bathroom?

OctoBoy: No.

Me: Then why are you holding your crotch like that?

OctoBoy: So I don't pee my pants.

I guess that makes sense when you're almost 3.

September 14, 2017

Hey Uncle <u>Charlie</u>, he likes it!

September 14, 2017

Looney Tunes aren't on TV any more because they're not PC. So I dug them up on youtube so OctoBoy wouldn't have to watch the wimpy crap on Disney and Nickelodeon. So far, I've been called a Filthy Varmint and told "Say yer prayers, ya long eared galoot!"

September 18, 2017

Rosie had a headache and had a problem swallowing the aspirin. We gave her a glass of water, which she spilled all over the kitchen. Mary Kay saw me wiping the water off the floor and jumped up and said "Papa, I'll get it. I don't want your back to hurt."

At a recent event that we had, someone had gone upstairs to breast feed their little one. Somehow, Mary Kay saw this and came back down and tells me "Papa, there's a lady upstairs milking her kid."

September 19, 2017

So today, OctoBoy and I went to Tops. He wanted to know if the one I go to his "liddle" carts like his Tops has. I asked him which Tops was his, and he looked at me, very matter of factly and said "The one on Twansit". (Not typo's btw) I went through the self check out, paid and started pushing the cart out of the store and he starts giggling and says "Papa, that mashine said 'Thank you for shopping at Tops. Have a nice day' My Tops doeshn't tell me dat when I go there!"

September 28, 2017

So today was this. Not Mary Kay, it was OctoBoy. I had a manly breakfast for him, and then we watched the TV show of The Incredible Hulk. He tells me he wants to watch Wocka Wocka Stwangew. I asked him where he saw it and he told me at home on TV. So I tried to find it. Nothing. I emailed Jill at work and she told me he wanted "Walker Texas Ranger". Silly me.

October 10, 2017

Ready to work!

October 24, 2017

So he's sitting across from me at the breakfast bar. A JG Wentworth commercial came on and he yells, "Go away! Nobody likes you!" He got up from his nap and was having a Tootsie Pop. I'm washing dishes and he says to me "Hewwo Moto".

November 23, 2017

OctoBoy's quote of the week: "Papa, I weely like your coffee filters". I guess that makes sense when you're "fwee".

November 28, 2017

So Junior was over yesterday and we had this conversation:

> Me: Dude, whats your favorite song?
>
> Him: (he sings Halleluiah) Me and Momma sing it in the car
>
> Me: Whats your favorite food?
>
> Him: Chicken Nuggets.
>
> Me: Cool. What's your favorite toy?
>
> Him: You.

I quit after that.

December 1, 2017

That'll work!

December 5, 2017

So yesterday it was this. We're sitting on the couch watching his new favorite old show, The Incredible Hulk (with Bill Bixby) from back in the late 70's

Junior: Papa, did you fawt?

Me: I did not!

Junior: Ok, I thought it wath me, but I wathn't thure.

December 6, 2017

"Gwamma, Come thee (see), me and Papa put up the Kwithmith Twee, but we didnt put the ordinanth on" Nope, no ammunition on our "Kwithmith Twee"!

December 27, 2017

So, the kids get dropped off this morning and right away, Junior wants me to put The Incredible Hulk on. I told him it wasn't on because they had some scary movie on with blood, guts and people getting killed left and right. Rosie pipes up and says "I bet Gramma would like it" I asked why she thought Gramma would like it" She said "Cause it sounds like Lifetime".

December 31, 2017

Me: Dude, don't pick your nose, that's gross!

Octoboy: But thewe's thtuff in thewe (there's stuff in there)

Me: Look at that, let me get a tissue.

Octoboy: Don't Wowwy (worry) Papa, ith gone.

Me: Where the hell did you wipe it"

Octoboy: I wouldn't do that Papa, I ate it.

BARF!

January 4, 2018

So yesterday was this one:

Octoboy: Papa, ith Uncoo Pat you bruvah? (Translation: Is Uncle Pat your brother))

Me: No, He's Gramma's brother.

Him: Why?

Me: Whaddya mean why? Because he is.

Mary Kay: No Norbie. Uncle Pat always says that he and Papa are brothers, but that they have different mothers. I never understood that either, but that's what he says.

January 5, 2018

I think he's praying for it to warm up! (The high was -5 today!)

January 31, 2018

I was having a bite to eat with Octo boy this morning. Had the news on in the background and he asks me "Papa, whath a Democwat?" Ya know? I couldn't answer him.

January 31, 2018

Me: Norbie, are you going to Aunt Jessie's on Sunday?

Norbie: Yep!

Me: Do you know why we're going there?

Norbie: Thure! It's Super Bowl and Uncle Mike's Brithday. Uncle Mike's Momma had to call the Super Bowl to see if he could be born on the Super Bowl and the Super Bowl said "Thure, that's ok"

Me: Oh, is that what happened?

Norbie: Yep!

Me: Who's gonna win the Super Bowl?

Norbie: Uncle Mike is cuz it's his brithday!

Ya can't make this stuff up.

February 9, 2018

Either I'm violating some kind of child labor laws, or making a new ad for Shark vacuums.

February 13, 2018

You can probably imagine the smile on my face when OctoBoy woke up from his nap and asked me if I would put on the Yellow Submarine video and he sat there, sang along and kept telling me "That's Wingo singing"! When that was over, he wanted the video where "Bo and Luke Duke make the General Lee fly and Woscoe goes in da lake!".

We've come a long way from Dora The Explorer and Barney!

February 20, 2018

Little Dude didn't want to nap. I knew he was tired, so I told him to close his eyes so I could count his eyelashes. He asked why I wasn't counting, so I started counting backward from 100. He was snoring by 36.

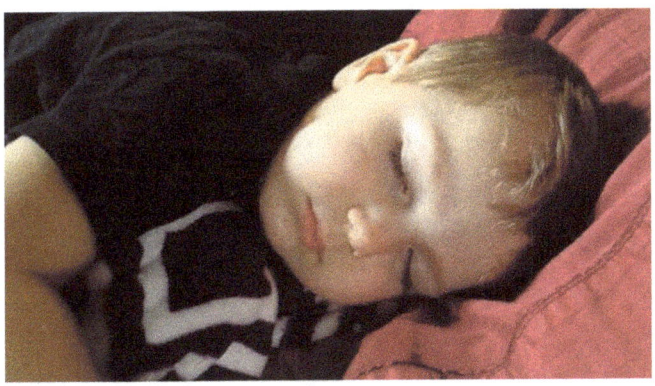

February 22, 2018

Rosie is a pain in the ass when it comes to feeding her and her eating habits are atrocious. I'm trying to get lunch the other day and suggesting pb&j, ham, salami, grilled cheese, fried egg, fluffernutter, the answer was no to all. OctoBoy was sitting next to her, eating his lunch and turns to her and says "Rosie, whaddya think thith ith? A fwiggin wethwant?" (translation: a friggin restaurant!)

I have no idea where he would have heard that.

February 28, 2018

"I'm goin to work by Uncle Pat. Could I have glass of wine in a cooler to take with me?"

March 2, 2018

After Rosie asked me how to spell about 15 words for something she's writing, I said "Man, I'm pretty smart. I should be a teacher". To which she replied "No way, no way, no way! You're WAY too hardcore and I would HATE to be in your class!"

So, I got that goin for me.

March 9, 2018

So Octo Boy walks in this morning watching The Beatles rooftop concert on Jill's phone. She told me "Dad, he's obsessed". I told her that I had nothing to do with it and she rolled her eyes and said "Yeah, I'll bet!" (I may have played a minor role) When I was making lunch, he tried snapping his fingers and started singing "Don't Wet Me Down" as only a 3 year old can do it

April 5, 2018

How does this work?

We look forward to them getting here. They drive us insane while we have them because we're not that young anymore. If we're lucky, they nap so that we can too. Then they wake up and havoc ensues. Shortly after, Mom picks them up and sanity is restored. But within an hour, we're calling to talk to them. We miss them and can't wait to do it all over again the next morning. And then it happens. Morning arrives and they trot in, proud as peacocks to give us the drawings that they made for us the night before, because they missed us as much as we missed them.

April 9, 2018

I was just told this by OctoBoy: "Papa. I had a bad dream. I was sleeping on your bottom stair. The was a monster, Santa and The Easter Bunny. The monster shooted Santa, but he got up. And then, and then, and then, the monster shooted The Easter Bunny. But he didn't get up. He got azzma. Then I waked up and turned into The Hulk and knocked down the building."

April 11, 2018

Another one for the book. Today he grabbed a stack of plastic coasters and said he was the mail man and was delivering invitations for "the pawty"

Me: What's the party for?

Octoboy: Kwithmith!

Me: A Christmas party now? It was just Easter.

Octoboy: Thure. And Thanta ith coming, and the Eather Bunny and the Inkwedibew Hulk and the Gwinch

Me: Oh good What about The Tooth Fairy, Mother Nature and Jack Frost?

Octoboy: No, thewe ithn't enough woom.

Me: But the Grinch can come? Remember last year? He went to the shrimp table and ate all the shrimp!

Octoboy: This yeaw, we havin cwab. All the grills hafta wear dwethes, thandles and pony tails.

Me: Really? What do I wear?

Octoboy: A thweat thuit. Now get weady before Batman and Joker get here!

Me: Did you invite the Duke Boys?

Octoboy: Nope. Only the General Lee. We got no more woom.

Me: Well what are Bo and Luke gonna say?

Octoboy: They thay "YEE HAAA!" papa. Thath when they jump the car!

Never a dull moment with that kid!

April 13, 2018

He wants me to put a 01 on the doors and a Rebel flag on the roof, just like The General Lee.

April 18, 2018

Ok, this actually just happened. OctoBoy said to Roni: You wanna come over to my house? We have adult toys you can play with."

April 18, 2018

What little kid doesn't dig a blanket fort with a robot mask made out of an old box?

April 22, 2018

Doug stopped in yesterday afternoon. Octoboy was here. Doug made a cup of coffee and Octoboy pointed his finger at him and said "Uncle Doug, the wules aawe, No shoes in the house!". Understandably, Doug laughed his ass off!

April 27, 2018

Norbie decided that "Gwamma needed an opawation for a bwoken fingew". This is how he prepped her. But he said she'd have to wait because "me and Pete hafta go out and catch thum bad guys."

May 5, 2018

Crazy little kid!

May 8, 2018

There is something seriously wrong at our humble abode. This home has always been filled with music of all kinds. Our basement is a full recording studio: guitars, drum kits, basses, mandolins, keyboards, laptops, monitors, soundboards, pedals etc. And yet suddenly, Roni starts singing the theme song for Paw Patrol.

May 9, 2018

I forgot about this one. Octoboy walked in Monday morning. He said "Hi Papa." So being a smart ass, I say "How do you do?" He looks at me with a puzzled face and says "How do I do what?"

May 9, 2018

Today was this:

> OctoBoy: Where did you get this house?
>
> Me: We bought it.
>
> Him: (eyes got real wide) Really????
>
> Me: Well of course
>
> Him: How did they fit it in the store?

I guess that makes sense when you're three.

May 11, 2018

Had to go to MASH this morning. Turns out I have an upper respiratory infection. But Doctor Norbie (Octoboy) had everything under control. He had me lay on the couch, put a blanket on me, covered me with couch pillows, put a coaster under my chin, put tissues all over my face and said "quiet Papa, I got this". I'll be damned if I don't feel better already!

May 16, 2018

OctoBoy: Can I have some M&Ms?

Me: Not now!

Him: Why?

Me: After lunch you can.

Him: Come on Man! Do me a solid!

I have no idea where he gets this stuff from!

May 21, 2018

OctoBoy is watching PAW Patrol. This episode is about pirates digging for buried treasure, so naturally, that's what he's making believe he's doing. But somehow, Shiver Me Timbers got translated to Send Me Some Tim Bits.

May 21, 2018

So this happened today: Octoboy had an incident with his sister. He came crying to me. I was in the garage having a cigarette. I put it out and said, "Cmon out Dude, lets talk". He gave me his hand, came out, sat on the same stair step that I was sitting on, leaned over and put his little chin on my knee and looked at me with those piercing blue eyes and said "Papa, I glad you my buddy". I told him, "Dude, **you're the best** buddy ever". Then he grabbed my other hand and said "Will you still be my buddy when I grow up like Uncle Chris and I'm a fireman or a Beatle?" Yep, that really happened.

May 30, 2018

With the Holiday weekend, Octoboy wasnt here for about 5 days. He walked in yesterday and very sheepishly waved to me and said "Hi Papa, wanna tickle me?"

Today, my mother had an "episode" so I flew over there at 7 AM. She's fine, but Roni told me he opened the back door 4 times, watching for me to pull in. He even asked Roni "What's taking him so long?" Little Dude is SO cool!

June 1, 2018

Me and Octo Boy hangin out watching the Incredible Hulk.

June 14, 2018

So the other day, my long time friend Beverly asked me how this guy got the name OctoBoy, but that she liked it better than FatBoy. Truth be told about the latter, he was huge. He was a lard. However, his hands were always fast.

One day, I was holding him and he pulled the chain off of my neck, knocked my glasses off and shoved a glass of wine out of my hand with one swipe. I said "Dude, it's like you have 8 hands!" Hence, "OctoBoy". But that is more of a persona than a name. I don't call him that. I call him "Dude" or "Little Kid". He's clearly not a FatBoy anymore, but he makes me laugh on a constant basis and follows me around like a puppy dog. I wouldn't want it any other way. Maybe I'll get him a Cape and Mask for Christmas.

June 18, 2018

I went out on the deck for a cigarette. We had the air on, so the slider was closed. I looked and saw Octo Boy laying on the dining room floor, waiting for me to come in. So this is me taking his picture, with my reflection in the glass outside.

June 28, 2018

So I'm trying to give OctoBoy a bit more leeway as he's getting older. First of which is taking a leak. He wants to be independent. I get that. But I also don't want to have him take that thing and spray piss all over. So I told him to take a leak the other day and told him he was on his own. He said "Papa, cwoth the doow tho I git pwivithy" (Close the door so I get privacy). I did. Heard the toilet flush, the seat slam and him washing his hands. Next thing I hear was BAM BAM BAM on the bathroom door and him screaming "PAPA, PAPA!" I ran to see what happened and opened the door to see him looking very embarassed and said "Sowwy, I tuend (turned) the light off befow I opened the doow and got scawed."

Glad I was there to save his life!

June 25, 2018

Me: Dude, where were you yesterday? You were gonna play with the band.

OctoBoy: I fogot to tell Momma to bwing me.

Me: Well, we waited for you as long as we could, and Doug said, "we can't wait any longer. We're already 2 minutes late" So we had to play without you.

OctoBoy: Papa, could I tell you a secret?

Me: Sure Dude. What's up?

He comes over to me, cups his hands around my ear and whispers: I wanted to play with the band, but I weally don't know how to play the kitar.

That's ok Kid. Someday.

July 9, 2018

Me: Mary Kay, whaddya want to be when you grow up?

Mary Kay: A Mom.

Me: What does it pay?

Mary Kay: $401,006.00

Me: Yeah, that sounds about what the job is worth. What are ya gonna name your kids? Simon? Theodore? Alvin?

Mary Kay: I don't know. But I DO know it won't be Hillary!

And I had nothing to do with it!

July 11, 2018

Mary Kay's words of wisdom for the day. Not bad for a six year old.

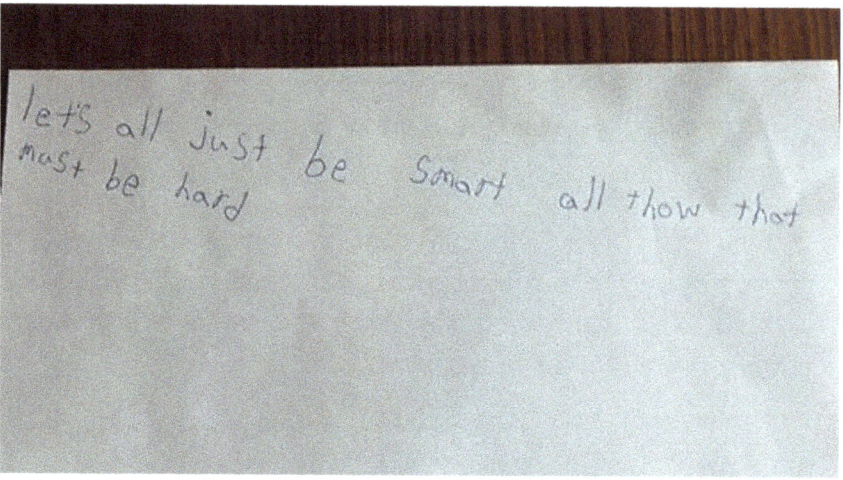

July 12, 2018

I'm watching a video today on how to fix the toilet. I hear some little feet coming down the hall and realize that OctoBoy woke up from his nap. He stands in front of me, still groggy and puts his arms up for me to pick him up, which is rare. He put his arms around my neck and his legs around my waist and squeezed with all his might and said "Papa, don't ever let go, ok?" Yep. I melted.

July 13, 2018

He prefers Gillette Foamy over Schick Gel.

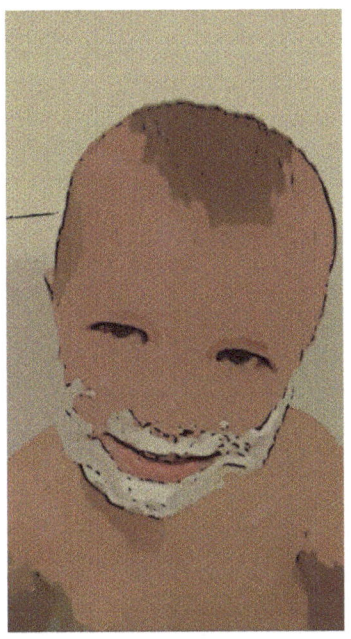

July 16, 2018

"Papa, do we need to wear shirts in Heaven?"

July 20, 2018

Helping Uncle John pick out boards at Lowes. He forgot his workerman boots and tool belt.

July 28, 2018

I went to pull my car in last night and heard click, click, click. My son in law Mike came over this morning and jumped it for me. I took it for a ride to charge the battery and noticed the dome light wasn't fading off. Reached up, pressed the button and off it went. Now I know how the battery died and I have a pretty good idea who turned it on, because it sure as hell wasn't me.

August 6, 2018

Me: Norbie, everyday, we watch the Paw Patrol help people and save people. They're doing all the hard work and we just sit here watching. Dontcha think we should help them save everybody?

Him: No!

Me: Why not? I'm sure they could use an extra hand

Him: No, they only on TV!

Me: Then let's get on TV!

Him: No, here's how it works. TV is TV and the world is the world. Does that make sense?

Silly me.

August 14, 2018

Octo Boy helping Uncle Billy Brown on the deck.

August 15, 2018

Octo Boy: Papa know what? We're goin camping this week

Me: Oh yeah? That's cool.

Him: But could you do me a favor?

Me: Sure little dude. What's up??

Him: Don't sell our house when we're gone, ok? We're coming back.

August 16, 2018

Another OctoBoy Story. (I'm gonna miss these days when he grows up!) Our new drummer, Joey brought his own electronic drum kit over the other day, so we moved <u>Doug's</u> over. Anyway, I went in the basement this morning to do some laundry and Junior follows me downstairs. Immediately, he noticed 2 drum kits, but didn't say anything. Instead, he walks over to my music stand that had a book open and a mic in front of it and asked "Papa, who's doing a reading?" I guess he pays attention in church.

Anyway, we go up to have breakfast and he tells me "I know why you got 2 drum sets" Me: "You do?" Then he says, very sheepishly "Yeah, you got them cuz you want me in you band. But I don't know how to play the drums. I only good at kitar. Not yours, it's too big. Just the one I got for Christmas"

August 21, 2018

So I took OctoBoy's wrist and was making him smack himself in the face with his own hand, saying "Quit hitting yourself in the face!", Then it was his turn. He took my hand and instead of smacking my face, he started hitting his own face with my hand and said "Quit hitting myself in the face!". I'm a bit worried about that boy.

August 25, 2018

The best part of today (if there is one at a funeral) was when it was over and I feel a little hand grasp mine. I look down and see Octo Boy (who obviously had been sleeping through the whole service) smiling at me with his mussed hair and bleary eyes saying "Hi Papa, I missed you. I got a shirt like you. I sit here with you, ok?"

August 31, 2018

Octoboy follows me into the basement this afternoon. He sees my 6 string next to the mic and music stand and asked if the band was here the other night. I told him it was just me and Doug and that we started recording a new song and that I played it and sang it first because I wrote it and no one else knew it yet. He looked at me kinda puzzled and wanted to know why everybody didn't play. So I told him, "what happens next is Doug will play his guitar, then Joe will play the drums and then Dave will play piano. Then we'll listen to it and make sure it sounds alright, and that's how you make a record".

He stood there staring at me, as innocent as could be and all he said was "Papa, what's a wecord?"

September 6, 2018

Getting ready to mail him to his Aunt for the Holidays.

September 7, 2018

It got to be nap time today. We went up to the loft, got on the love seat and OctoBoy started jumping on me like we always do. Playing, crunching, tickling, laughing. But I said "Dude, I didn't sleep too good last night. I need a nap too". He jumped up and said "Dont wowwy Papa, I take care of you". He ran and got a pillow and a blanket and put them on me, laid next to me, held my hand and fell asleep. These things I post don't even equal how cool and funny this little dude is!

September 7, 2018

Last week, I was peeling potatoes to make German Potato Salad for a party we had to go to. Naturally, I had Curious George trying to figure out what I was doing

Him: Are you gonna cook those potatoes?

Me: Yep, peel em, cut em up and then boil em!

Hi: Then what?

Me: Then you cook them all together in a big pot with vinegar, onions and bacon and boy, is that good!

Him: But I'm a boy! Don't cook me!

September 10, 2018

"Nobody tickled me at School today Papa. Wanna tickle me?"

September 10, 2018

First week of school is behind us, but the weather is still warm. When they all got home from school, we were sitting on the deck and they were having freezie pops. Somehow, Roni, Rosie and Mary Kay got into a conversation about pedicures, which morphed into talking about foot massages. At her previous job, Roni used to go to China for two weeks every year and she was telling the girls how fantastic a Chinese foot massage was and that no one can do a foot massage like Chinese women. As they're talking about it, the girls are fascinated and Roni gets up and says "Hang on Rosie, let me go get something for you from my closet" and walked into the house.

Rosie turns her head and looks at me, her eyes as big a saucers and with total innocence says "Papa? Gramma keeps a Chinese person in her closet?"

September 13, 2018

> Me: Norbie, who ya gonna vote for today?
>
> Him: You!

Smart kid!

September 18, 2018

He comes walking into the living room carrying this little doll in his arms and says "Papa, do you like my little baby? She likes having her head crushed."

That was disturbing on two different levels.

September 20, 2018

OctoBoy and I had lunch at McDonalds today (which sucked)

I asked him what he wanted to be when he grew up. I knew what he was gonna say because I've asked him that dozens of times before, but he added something new this time:

"I gonna be a fiweman. But not just a fiweman, I wanna dwive the twuck. But you won't see me do it. You and Gwamma will be in Heaven"

There was an older couple behind us and I could hear them trying to quiet their laughs. When we left, the guy looked at me and said "See ya there!"

September 21, 2018

About 2 weeks ago, I took OctoBoy for a walk through the "woods" in our back yard. I showed him the trees that the wood peckers got in the spring and showed him the 5 holes they made and the dead roots. And because of how tall it was, a good wind would bring it down and it could hit the house.

Fast forward to today. I walked in from the garage and saw him staring into "the woods". He heard the weather forecast on the radio while we were driving around. I asked what he was looking at and I got this: "Papa, that wind is gonna knock that twee into our house. You and Gwamma can come live with uth, but we gotta fix the house. Call Uncle Charlie, Uncle Doug, Roberto and Sebastian. We gotta get a lotta wood to fix this. You get your tools and take me home to get mine, cuz we gotta work". I'm trying hard not to piss my pants from laughing, but I said "What about Trisha?" "No she's a girl. We need strong men. She can stay inside with Gwamma and Aunt Connie to make food for us worker men"

I'm surprised he didn't just ask me to call the Paw Patrol.

September 26, 2018

Me: Dude, we're running late. Let's just grab something at McDonalds. What do you want?

Him: A bwekfist sanwich, Chicken nuggets and a cheesebewger

Me: Pick one.

Him: I did. I picked those ones.

September 27, 2018

So our sewer is clogged out at the curb. I'm explaining to OctoBoy how the plumber is going to come, bring the machine out of his truck and put a very long hose down the sewer pipe to break up the clog.

He says: "And then what? The Teenage Mutant Ninja Turtles grab the hose?"

September 12, 2018

I guess this was a bad idea. I went to pick up OctoBoy from his first day at Saint Mary's Pre K. All the adults were crammed in the front hall waiting for the nose pickers to come out. They bring them out one at a time, say their name and wait for them to be claimed. Then they bring him out and say "Norbie". I had to look to see if it was the right Norbie and when I saw it was him, I said "I'll take that one". Well that teacher just stared at me and held on to him until she could see that he knew me.

October 10, 2018

Another OctoBoy Original from the ride home from school today: "Mother Nature and Mother Mary are very special mothers Papa. Did you know that Mother Mary is Jesus's mother? And did you know that God is Jesus's dad? And Mother Nature is Jesus's I think that's his aunt. I think."

And this is where I'm stopping this. Little snippets from the last six years that I am very grateful that I documented. I actually read some of them to the kids the other day and they laughed so hard that they had tears rolling down their cheeks and in total disbelief that they actually said those things.

And in closing, I will leave you with the words to a song that OctoBoy was proud as punch to sing for me the other day when he got home from school:

"Wo, wo, wo you boat, gentwy down the stweam. Mewwy, mewwy, mewwy, mewwy, wife's about a dweam."

The End